i.

i am the running girl

i am the running girl

by **arnold adoff**

pictures by
ronald himler

*811
A DO
7822*

harper & row, publishers
new york   hagerstown
san francisco   london

Library of Congress Cataloging in Publication Data
Adoff, Arnold.
    I am the running girl.

    SUMMARY: A young girl describes the joy and pride
that running gives her.
    1. Running—Juvenile poetry. [1. Running—Poetry.
2. American poetry] I. Himler, Ronald. II. Title.
PZ8.3.A233Iam   811'.5'4   78-14083
ISBN 0-06-020094-4
ISBN 0-06-020095-2 lib. bdg.

7822

for my running girl
        leigh
                hamilton
        adoff
and
her sisters
   in spikes

my name is rhonda

and i am the youngest
of three sisters

poppa plays tennis

                          and my sisters swim
and jog and walk
but
    i am the running girl
                          in the family

            momma used to run

            when she was in school
                          in this town

            now i am following

each morning early
                    before school

momma is on the bike
and i am in my running
                    shoes
along the sidewalks
  of this
          side
  of town

                    when i get tired

                              or my legs cramp
                              or my ankle
                                        hurts
            i ride
                    and momma walks along

                    telling strategies

in my head
           i am the panther on the plain

in my head
           i am the fox in the field
in my head
           i am faster
    than the animals

pushing
      against
the
air

after a while
    there is no momma or bike
or my moving
    legs

i am only two feet banging
  onto the concrete
      and blacktop
       streets
of this early morning
     run

and i am tired to my toes
  when we get home

i play soccer and basketball
                    and practice
the running long jump
                    in the backyard pit

but i am the running girl
    i am the girl running
                    for myself
and for my team
                    and for the winning

inside the shouting of the crowd
                    i hear my name

each time i race
        i race the girls on the track
and the clock
    in my
      head

and in my
        head are other girls i don't know
  in chicago and new york
              or california

on my school track i stretch my legs
      and stretch for magic
                medals
      in some future games
                and
race the other girls
        i don't even know

sisters

i read the sports pages and the magazines
and listen to the women
                    on their interviews

at the track   i hold my faded   uniform
against the brand-new shirts and pants
          the boys are wearing
and stand up   to the staring

coach says
          we are running   for the right to run
          and next year they will spend money
          on new uniforms before the season
                              starts
and other coaches will remember
our names and times against any
                         one
if we remember
          we are running for
                    the fun
               and for the right
          to run

most of our meets are girls
against girls

but sometimes i run against
boys
and they don't scare me
on
or off the track

when i run well
they can pat me
on the back
and say
good
race

last year i was a sprinter
                       and ran short dashes
and didn't know how far
          i could go

then this winter my legs began to grow
and i became stronger
                and i could run
                         long
         distances
and race a longer
         time
             around the track
             past the place
where it would begin
        to hurt

after

afternoons of running over country roads
and jogging around the track
to practice
       running form
          for hours
one
day it is april and we must be ready
       for the season
          to begin
i am ready

at the meet i must warm up slowly

    with   jumping jack exercises
       and jogs around the track

i have to loosen my legs
    and tighten my mind
    and think
about
    the
    run

there is always too much time
between the races

i find my place   and wait
for my name to be called

i can rest on the grass
and stretch my legs
out
and do the running
over
and
over

in my head
i have the plans
and strategies
and
a picture of the breaking
tape

i have won

just before my race

i say hello
to the other
                girls
and
sip some orange
                juice
and
   water

we smile
        and lie
        a little
about
   experience
and
   time
and
   line up
        in our l a n e s

waiting for the gun

880

get a good start and stay
in the pack
            around the first
                        turn
and stay with the
                leader
after the first
            time
        around the track

and stay with the leader
until it's time to try
            and get ahead
until it's time to
            kick

thinking to kick

      when i am running right
      and the
            long muscles
      of my legs are
             moving
      long and loose
        and my head is tight
            into the race

      and the first time around
        was fast enough to keep up
        but not too fast
               to make me
      use up all
        my strength

i am near the shoulder
                    of the girl
                    in the lead

and maybe this lead girl
                         looks
                              back
for a second
to see if i am still
          on her shoulder

then my eyes
tell her
          good
          bye

kick

i can switch to my fastest speed
because i can press that button
in
my brain

and the power of orange juice
and candy bars
and morning runs
with momma
slides down my throat
and stomach
to
my legs

and i can pump and pump
around
the final turn
to the tape

home

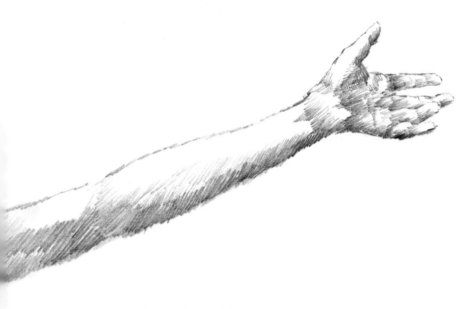

the other girls
        fall far   behind
        like a dream story

and the lead girl is moving
    in her place
    is standing
        still

i open my legs wide and stride once
                 for her two steps

i am making the breeze
i am
    the breeze

i am the race

the end

    is past the tape at the finish line
    and i am bending to the ground
              out of breath
              and strength

    the coach is shouting
           i have broken   three
                  minutes
   for the first time
   but i am out of
          time

    i have no bones
    i have no legs
    i have no
          stomach that will stay
            where it began
   but i have won

after the race

                    my friends hug me
the way i hug them after their
                              races

while i am running they are all
        a blur of faces
                        as i come around
                              the turns

but
now   there is my sister
        there is my father
and
    my momma taking
                        pictures
        of my dirty
                face

i am the running girl

        there are walking girls
           and jogging
    girls
          in the streets

    girls who ride their
               bikes
    and hike along brown
    country roads with
             brothers
    and their friends
    and pull wild flowers
         for their hair
    but

i am the running girl
    there in the moving day
    and i cannot stop to
            say
    hello

Designed by Kohar Alexanian
Set in 12 pt. Alphatype Claro Medium
Composed by Royal Composing Room
Printed by Rae Publishing Co., Inc.
Bound by Publishers Book Bindery, Inc.
HARPER & ROW, PUBLISHERS, INC.